Soul Walk

Before, During, & Afterlife

Companion Workbook

Reflections, Practices, and Realignment for the Mind, Body, and Spirit

Sophia C. Russell

Cover and interior design by Sophia C. Russell
ISBN 979-8-9998343-0-0
Printed in the United States of America
First Edition
Published by *Prosperity House Publishing*

This workbook is intended for informational purposes only. It does not substitute professional advice or treatment. The author and publisher disclaim any liability arising from the use or misuse of this material. Readers are encouraged to use discernment and seek qualified guidance as needed.

This workbook is a companion to the original book *Soul Walk: Before, During, and Afterlife*. It is intended for personal growth, education, and reflection. The author assumes no responsibility for any outcomes resulting from the exercises or interpretations presented herein.

*Publication of Prosperity House Publishing, a Black woman-owned independent press dedicated to amplifying spiritual, holistic, and metaphysical voices from diverse communities.

For permissions or bulk purchase inquiries, please contact:

Prosperity House Publishing
Dallas, Texas, USA
prosperityhouse.co
help.prosperity@gmail.com
469-868-6061

"When I remain open, wonderful things express themselves through me"

—Allee Willis (Iconic Songwriter, Producer, Artist)

Welcome!

This companion workbook was created as a sacred space for reflection, integration, and deeper connection with the journey explored in the book *Soul Walk: Before, During, and Afterlife*. Whether you're walking through a personal awakening, navigating hidden truths, or seeking clarity beyond religious tradition, these pages are here to support you. I crafted each section to offer you thoughtful prompts and space to process your experiences, so take your time with each section, allowing the insights to unfold naturally. Some chapters may speak to you quickly, while others may invite you to linger for a week or even two. There is no rush—move at the rhythm of your own soul, trusting that each pause and reflection is part of the journey. May this workbook guide you inward—to remember, realign, and reclaim the wisdom of your soul.

–Sophia

CONTENTS

✎ Journal Space:

✎ Journal Space:

SECTION 1: Waking Up from Spiritual Amnesia
(*Corresponds with Soul Walk Chapters 1–3*)

Amnesia is defined as "a partial or total loss of memory." Spiritually, many of us are living under this condition — having forgotten who we truly are and why we came. Though we agreed to this forgetting before entering the human experience, we didn't fully grasp how disorienting it would be to create and evolve while under the influence of the world around us. Yet this forgetting serves a purpose. It is through the journey of remembering that our soul expands. Every moment of awareness, every spark of inner knowing, is a step toward awakening.

Core Insights

- Many of us are born into systems of belief without questioning their origin.
- Spiritual amnesia can cause us to live disconnected from our soul's original knowing.
- Transitioning out of rigid religious frameworks often requires courage, loss, and self-trust.

Guided Reflections

1. *Inherited Belief vs. Inner Knowing*

  - What belief systems were handed to you by family, culture, or tradition?
  - Which of these beliefs have you questioned or outgrown?
  - How did you first notice your spirit resisting or awakening?

2. *Soul Shifts* moments of enlightened awareness, or a profound shift in a core belief

  - Recall a moment when something in your worldview shifted.
  - What triggered this moment? How did it feel?

3. *Spiritual Permission*

  - Have you ever felt like you needed permission to explore outside your inherited faith?
  - What would it look like to give yourself that permission now?

✎ Journal Space:

_____

_____

_____

Soul Work *Assignments*

1. **Timeline of Awakening:** On a blank page or in your journal, sketch a timeline of your spiritual awakening.

2. **Letter to My Younger Self:** Write a compassionate letter to your past self — the one who first began to question, awaken, or grieve the loss of old beliefs.

3. **Soul Walk Check-In:** Complete the following sentence starters:

- "My soul is most alive when…"
- "The question I keep returning to is…"
- "I used to believe ____, but now I understand…"

✎ Journal Space:

_____

_____

_____

_____

_____

_____

_____

_____

Spiritual Practice Prompt

The Mirror Practice: Each morning for 3 days, stand before a mirror and say out loud:
"I am not broken. I am remembering. My soul knows the way."
Write down how you feel after each day.

✎ Journal Space:

_____

_____

_____

_____

_____

_____

SECTION 2: Listening to the Soul's Call
(Corresponds with Soul Walk Chapters 4–6)

Your soul is always speaking — not in words, but in symbols, feelings, and quiet nudges. In a world full of noise and expectation, it can be difficult to hear that inner voice clearly. But beneath the distractions, your soul is gently calling you back to your truth. The more still you become, the louder it speaks. Listening is not about effort — it's about trust, presence, and the willingness to follow a knowing that doesn't need proof.

Core Insights

- The soul communicates in symbols, intuition, and inner knowing rather than logic alone.
- Ignoring the soul's promptings can create inner tension or even illness.
- Tuning into the soul's voice requires stillness, trust, and discernment.

Guided Reflections

1. *Inner Promptings*
   - What signs or sensations do you experience when your soul is speaking?
   - How often do you trust these impressions versus override them?

2. *Conflicting Voices*
   - What are some external voices (family, culture, fear) that drown out your inner guidance?
   - How can you lovingly set boundaries within yourself that helps to address those influences?

3. *Knowing Without Proof*
   - Have you ever "just known" something without external evidence?
   - What happened when you followed or ignored that knowing?

✎ Journal Space:

_____

_____

_____

_____

_____

Soul Work *Assignments*

1. **Soul Listening Journal:** For 5 days, take 5 quiet minutes each morning. Write down the first feeling, image, or thought that arises.

2. **The Soul Says...:** Write a short stream-of-consciousness passage beginning with: "My soul wants me to know..."

3. **Symbol Watch:** Choose a symbol you feel drawn to. Track when and how it appears over the next week. What do you intuitively sense it means?

✎ Journal Space:

_____
_____
_____
_____
_____
_____
_____
_____
_____
_____
_____
_____
_____

Spiritual Practice Prompt

Soul Stillness: Each evening before bed, place your hands over your heart and ask aloud:
"What is it you want me to hear?"
Breathe deeply, listen, and journal your impressions.

✎ Journal Space:

_____
_____
_____
_____
_____

✎ Journal Space:

✎ Journal Space:

SECTION 3: Walking Between Worlds
(Corresponds with Soul Walk Chapters 7–9)

Some of us live with one foot in the seen world, and one in the unseen. You may feel things others don't, or sense layers of reality beyond what's visible. This ability isn't confusion — it's remembrance. To walk between worlds is to be a bridge, honoring both the physical and the non-physical as equally real. Your sensitivity is not a flaw; it is a gift calling you into deeper alignment.

Core Insights

- You are a bridge between non-physical and physical realities.
- Sensitivity, intuition, and multidimensional awareness are natural gifts.
- Many who walk between worlds feel 'different' — your difference is divine.

Guided Reflections

1. *Between Realities*
   - Where do you feel torn between the seen and unseen?
   - How do you navigate practical life while honoring your spiritual sensitivity?

2. *Spiritual Gifts*
   - What gifts have you discovered (intuition, dreams, energy perception)?
   - How did others respond when you shared them?

3. *Integration*
   - What would full integration of your spiritual and human self look like?
   - What might shift if you stopped hiding your multidimensional nature?

✎ Journal Space:

_____

_____

_____

_____

_____

_____

Soul Work *Assignments*

1. **Bridging Letter**: Write a letter from your spiritual self to your everyday self. Let it guide, affirm, and comfort.

2. **Day in the Life:** Imagine and describe a day where you feel fully aligned in both your spiritual and earthly identities.

3. **Anchoring Practice:** Identify one habit that grounds you. Commit to using it when feeling overwhelmed by unseen energies.

✎ Journal Space:

_____

_____

_____

_____

_____

_____

_____

_____

Spiritual Practice Prompt

Two-Worlds Walk: Place one hand on your heart, one on your belly. Say:
"I honor both my Spirit and my form."
Breathe into this union and journal how it feels.

✎ Journal Space:

_____

_____

_____

_____

_____

_____

_____

SECTION 4: Sacred Memory and the Soul's Blueprint
(Corresponds with Soul Walk Chapters 10–12)

Your soul carries memory that stretches beyond this lifetime. Some of what you feel — the callings, the fears, even the patterns — may not begin with you, but through you. Whether from past lives, ancestral echoes, or soul contracts, your blueprint is rich with purpose. Remembering isn't about getting it "right," but about recognizing what wants to be healed, reclaimed, or completed through you.

Core Insights

- You carry ancient memories within your soul's field.
- Your challenges may relate to past lives, ancestral echoes, or soul contracts.
- Awakening involves decoding what you're here to heal, reclaim, or activate.

Guided Reflections

1. *Soul Contracts*

   - Have you felt destined to meet certain people or repeat certain patterns?
   - What purpose might these serve in your evolution?

2. *Ancestral Influence*

   - What beliefs, traumas, or strengths do you feel you've inherited?
   - How do you relate to your lineage — with pride, pain, curiosity?

3. *Past-Life Resonance*

   - Do any time periods, places, or symbols feel especially familiar?
   - What do you intuit *or sense* that they are connected to in your soul's story?

✎ Journal Space:

_____

_____

_____

_____

_____

_____

_____

Soul Work *Assignments*

1. **Soul Timeline:** Draw a spiral or timeline of your spiritual memories. Include past life impressions, ancestral moments, or turning points in this life.

2. **Contract Rewrite:** Write a symbolic "contract" of your soul's purpose in this life. What themes are you here to explore, heal, and embody?

3. **Ancestral Altar:** Create a small space with objects or symbols to honor your ancestors. Light a white candle, close your eyes, and say: "Thank you. I remember."

✎ Journal Space:

_____

_____

_____

_____

_____

_____

_____

_____

Spiritual Practice Prompt

Memory Meditation: Close your eyes and ask:
"What memory wants to awaken in me today?"
Breathe slowly and journal any images, feelings, or phrases that come.

✎ Journal Space:

_____

_____

_____

_____

_____

_____

_____

SECTION 5: The Language of Energy
(Corresponds with Soul Walk Chapters 13–15)

Everything is energy — not just your body, but your thoughts, emotions, and environment. The soul responds to vibration more than logic, and healing often happens at the unseen level first. When you learn to sense and shift energy, you begin to change your experience from the inside out. This is the language your soul speaks fluently. You are simply learning how to listen.

Core Insights

- Everything is energy — thoughts, emotions, intentions, and environments.
- Your soul responds to frequency more than words or logic.
- Healing often requires shifting the energetic story beneath the physical symptoms.

Guided Reflections

1. *Energy Awareness*

   - How do different spaces, people, or experiences affect your energy?
   - What drains you? What restores you?

2. *Chakras & Emotions*

   - Are there specific body areas where you hold tension or pain?
   - What emotions or past events might be stored there?
   - If you need assistance understanding the Chakras visit this site
     https://www.healthline.com/health/fitness-exercise/7-chakras

3. *Frequency Check*

   - What practices raise your vibration?
   - What choices lower your vibration, and how can you shift them?

✎ Journal Space:

_____

_____

_____

_____

_____

Soul Work *Assignments*

1. **Energy Journal**: Each day this week, track your energy highs and lows. What seems to influence them?

2. **Chakra Scan:** Lie down and bring your attention slowly through each chakra center. Journal impressions or blockages you sense.

3. **Frequency Reset:** Choose one uplifting song, movement, or mantra and use it each day to reset your frequency.

✎ Journal Space:

_____

_____

_____

_____

_____

_____

_____

_____

_____

_____

Spiritual Practice Prompt

Energy Bath: Sit quietly for a few minutes and imagine a stream of golden light flowing through your body. See it washing away dense energy. End with gratitude.

✎ Journal Space:

_____

_____

_____

_____

_____

SECTION 6: Sacred Disruption
(Corresponds with Soul Walk Chapters 16–18)

There are times when life unravels — not to punish, but to realign. Disruption can feel chaotic, yet it often clears what no longer serves your soul's path. When things fall apart, something deeper is often falling into place. Be mindful how you interpret these events. Lower emotions such as fear, anxiety, anger, and doubt can often prolong them. Trust that even in loss or uncertainty, your soul is still guiding the way.

Core Insights

- Sometimes things must fall apart to realign with your soul's truth.
- Spiritual growth can at times look like confusion, loss, or uncertainty.
- Disruption can be divine — it clears what no longer serves.

Guided Reflections

1. *Sacred Chaos*

   - What parts of your life have unraveled recently?
   - Could this be clearing space for something new?

2. *Loss & Letting Go*

   - What or who have you released — willingly or not?
   - What has this loss taught you about trust, control, or faith?

3. *Emergence*

   - What parts of you are emerging from the disruption?
   - What do you now know that you didn't before?

✎ Journal Space:

_____

_____

_____

_____

_____

Soul Work *Assignments*

1. **Rubble to Roots:** On a blank page, draw or list things that have 'fallen apart.' Then beneath each, note what roots or growth they've created.

2. **Letter to the Storm:** Write to the disruption as if it were a teacher. What did it come to show you?

3. **New Ground:** Identify one new value, boundary, or truth you've gained through this process.

✎ Journal Space:

_____

_____

_____

_____

_____

_____

_____

_____

Spiritual Practice Prompt

Resilience Ritual: Light a candle and say:
"Even when it breaks me open, I remain sacred."
Sit with that flame for 5 minutes in stillness.

✎ Journal Space:

_____

_____

_____

_____

_____

_____

✎ Journal Space:

✎ Journal Space:

SECTION 7: Soul Relationships & Divine Mirrors
(Corresponds with Soul Walk Chapters 19–21)

Every relationship is a mirror reflecting aspects of your inner world — your wounds, your gifts, your growth. Some people come to comfort, others to challenge, but all serve your evolution. As you awaken, you begin to see each connection not just as personal, but as part of a soul-level agreement to help you remember who you are.

Core Insights

- Relationships are soul classrooms — not just sources of comfort or pain.
- Everyone you meet reflects something in you: fear, love, patterns, potential.
- True healing often happens in the mirror of another.

Guided Reflections

1. *Patterns in People*

   - What types of people do you attract repeatedly?
   - What do those relationships teach you about your beliefs or wounds?

2. *Soul Connections*

   - Who has impacted you the most spiritually, and why?
   - Do you believe in soulmates or soul contracts?

3. *The Mirror Principle*

   - What current relationship is challenging you most?
   - What is it revealing about how you see or treat yourself?

✎ Journal Space:

_____

_____

_____

_____

_____

_____

Soul Work *Assignments*

1. *Mirror Journal:* Write about a recent interaction that triggered you. What old wound or story did it touch?

2. *Soul Letter:* Write a letter to someone who deeply affected your soul's growth. It is not necessary to give this letter to the person, if you feel called to give it, then do so. Just remember this is more about your own growth.

3. *Relational Reset:* Identify one relationship where you can show up with more authenticity and less fear.

✎ Journal Space:

_____

_____

_____

_____

_____

_____

_____

_____

Spiritual Practice Prompt

The Mirror Gaze: Gaze into your own eyes in a mirror for 3 minutes. Whisper,
"I see you. I love you. I forgive you."
Write about what arises.

✎ Journal Space:

_____

_____

_____

_____

_____

_____

SECTION 8: Realigning with Purpose
(Corresponds with Soul Walk Chapters 22–23)

Purpose is not just about what you do — it's about how you show up, how you love, and how you align with your soul's truth. Often, purpose is revealed slowly, in quiet callings and small steps. As you reconnect with your essence, life begins to feel more meaningful, and the path ahead becomes clearer.

Core Insights

- Your soul came here for a reason — even if it's still unfolding.
- Purpose is not just what you do; it's who you are and how you show up.
- The more you align with your truth (or passion), the more purposeful life becomes.

Guided Reflections

1. *Inner Compass*

  - What makes you feel most alive or at peace?
  - How does your body react when you're aligned vs. misaligned?

2. *Soul Gifts*

  - What are your natural passions, strengths or callings?
  - Where do others come to you for help or wisdom?

3. *Divine Timing*

  - What dreams are you holding for the future?
  - What is one small step you can take today toward one of your dreams?

✎ Journal Space:

_____

_____

_____

_____

_____

_____

Soul Work *Assignments*

1. *Soul Map:* Create a visual or written map of where you've been and where your soul feels drawn next.

2. *Purpose Declaration:* Write a 1-page 'I am here to…' statement that reflects your soul's purpose.

3. *Sacred Step:* Choose one thing to do this week that brings you joy, meaning, or alignment — no matter how small.

✎ Journal Space:

_____

_____

_____

_____

_____

_____

_____

_____

Spiritual Practice Prompt

Light Walk: Take a walk in silence, asking:
"What is mine to do now?"
Observe what you notice in your body, nature, and thoughts. Journal it afterward.

✎ Journal Space:

_____

_____

_____

_____

_____

_____

_____

✎ Journal Space:

_____

_____

_____

_____

_____

_____

_____

_____

_____

_____

_____

_____

_____

_____

_____

_____

_____

_____

_____

_____

_____

✎ Journal Space:

SECTION 9: Final Blessing Page

Living a soul-led life is not a one-time shift — it's a daily practice. Some days you'll feel deeply connected, and other days you may forget. That's okay. Growth is not linear, and healing unfolds in layers. Even after completing this workbook, you may find yourself returning to certain pages, questions, or practices — and when you do, they will meet you where you are. Be gentle with yourself. Consistency matters more than perfection. You're not behind — you're becoming.

Your Soul's Commitment

As you complete this journey, take a quiet moment to listen inward. What is your soul asking of you now? What truths are ready to be lived more fully? This is your invitation to write down a few intentions, affirmations, or soul-aligned goals that feel true for this next season of your life. You don't need to have it all figured out — just begin with honesty and heart. This is your sacred agreement with yourself.

✎ **My soul-centered commitments:**

- _____

- _____

- _____

- _____

Soul Blessing for the Journey Ahead

May you walk in remembrance of who you truly are.
May the light you've reclaimed illuminate your every step.
May your questions birth deeper wisdom, not fear.
May you trust your inner knowing more than the noise of the world.
May your soul feel held, honored, and heard — in this life and beyond.

As you continue your walk, may you know:
You are never alone. You are never lost. **You** are the light you've been seeking.

✎ Journal Space:

✎ Journal Space: